Monkey Chinese Horoscope 2025

By

IChingHunFùyǒu FengShuisu

Table of Contents

Introduce

The character of people born in the year of the MONKEY

People born this year have smart, cunning personalities that are hidden behind cuteness. They talk because they are cute, they are fun-loving, they have intelligence that is easy to teach, and they can learn quickly. People born in this year are very attractive and charming. They are usually very interested in social gatherings. However, they rarely hide their own emotions because everything will come out on their faces as they get to know each other. People born in this year are excellent problem solvers. If you have a problem, they will always offer to assist you, will be a good listener, and will always suggest the appropriate words. Curiosity drives people born this year to constantly learn. The disadvantage of the Year of the Monkey is that there is sometimes a lack of reason. And you're ready to paint a picture for yourself and others to believe in everything people born in the Year of the Monkey do. Staying is always the best option. People born in the Year of the Monkey are perceived as selfish, opportunistic, and cunning by some. People born in this year are uninterested. Friends born in this year are devoted and loyal. Aside from that, you're a sweet-tempered but repulsive lover who fades quickly.

Strength:
You value unity and enjoy resolving problems for others.

Weaknesses:
You enjoy teasing others, and as a result, you are looked down upon; don't think twice before acting.

Love:
People born this year have a lot of love because they are cute, talkative, and talkative. In addition to extramarital affairs, they frequently manage their charms when they like someone and get to know each other without hesitation. People born this year as boyfriends look cute because they are calm, always consider the

feelings of others, don't like to fuss, frequently talk to each other for a reason, and if they still don't agree with someone, they will ask to be together for a long time. Proof but if you find the person who likes you the most, just getting along with each other is enough.

Suitable Career:

People born in the Year of the Monkey are thought to be of the golden element. Architects, actors, artists, handicrafts, brokers, consultants, banks, and opening a shop selling construction materials are all professions that promote and suit your destiny. Working in metallurgy, machinery, selling automobiles or automobile accessories, iron ore, industrial plants, ceramics, selling jewelry, or even agricultural work Real estate development is a lucrative business for people born in the year of the Monkey.

Year of the MONKEY (Water) | (1944) & (2004)

" Monkey in the tree" is a person born in the year of the MONKEY at the age of 81 years (1944) and 21 years (2004)

Overview

For senior people in this age group, this year is another year that you should take care of your health strictly because it may cause problems, especially in terms of food and drink. You should take care of your health, do not eat spicy food, and avoid food that is high in fat. If you feel any abnormalities, you should see a doctor for regular check-ups. In addition, you should not interfere with other people's problems, especially by being intrusive with your children and grandchildren. If anyone visits you, you should give them blessings and precepts, and you will be respected by your family and close friends. At the beginning of the year, you should find time to pay respect and ask for blessings from Tai Sui to be safe from bad luck and disasters and have good health.

For people in the age group of 21, because they have received auspicious power, this year for those who have started working, this year your work and business will find a patron. Your education will progress. However, all work activities must be more diligent and determined, and you must develop yourself by always adding new skills and knowledge to keep up with all the changes to find smoothness and be able to get through it. However, during the year, you will be harassed by the evil stars, which will cause various problems and obstacles. Therefore, the best way is not to interfere in matters that are not your business. Also, be careful of accidents during work and travel. Be careful of people who slander you.

If friends invite you to go to a place that will easily lead you to vices, you should refuse and know how to control your temper. Do not get angry when provoked or do anything without thinking because if you have a problem, it will be too late to regret it later. And since both of these horoscopes will be affected by the clashing power of Tai Sui, at the beginning of the year, you should find time to pay respect to Tai Sui to ask for his blessings to protect you from dangers and misfortunes.

Career and Business

For young people, this year, whether you are working or doing business, you will progress. Or if you are studying at the university level, this year you have the right to study both domestically and internationally and will have a good future in a good position. Therefore, if you increase your determination and improve your skills, you will be more successful and have a good foundation for the future. Especially the months when your studies and career are outstanding and progressing are the 2nd Chinese month (March 5 – April 3), the 3rd Chinese month (April 4 – May 4), the 5th Chinese month (June 5 – July 6), and the 9th Chinese month (October 8 – November 6). The months when your studies and career will be obstructed and not smooth are the 1st Chinese month (February 3 – March 4), the 4th Chinese month (May 5 – June 4), the 7th Chinese month

(August 7 – September 6), and the 10th Chinese month (November 7 – December 6). In any work, You must follow the rules of society and the law. You must be extra careful in your work and investment during this period because you may be deceived or taken advantage of. Please be careful.

Financial

This year, your financial horoscope is in deficit. There are many expenses but your income is decreasing. It can be said that you have a chance to be in the red almost every month. If you cannot find a way to earn more money, it would be better for you to reduce your expenses to balance your finances or else you have to use your savings to make ends meet. You should save on things that you do not need to spend or spend. You have to save up and prepare for unexpected expenses that will reduce your liquidity even more, especially during the 1st Chinese Month (February 3 - March 4), the 4th Chinese Month (May 5 - June 4), the 7th Chinese Month (August 7 - September 6), and the 10th Chinese Month

(November 7 - December 6). During these periods, you should not lend money to others or accept guarantees. You should not gamble or take risks. You should not do any business that is likely to be against the law or immoral. Be careful of the danger of falling victim to fraud. The months when your finances flow smoothly are the 2nd Chinese month (5 March – 3 April), the 3rd Chinese month (4 April – 4 May), the 5th Chinese month (5 June – 6 July), and the 9th Chinese month (8 October – 6 November).

Family

This year, your family will have both good and bad things mixed in it. Even though you have good energy, you will also find bad stars staring at you, which will usually affect the safety of your family members and your involvement in lawsuits. However, if you have an auspicious event in your home, it will help alleviate bad things. However, you should be careful about the health problems and illnesses of the elderly. In addition, you should be careful of your juniors or servants who will cause you trouble, especially during the 1st Chinese Month

(February 3 - March 4), the 4th Chinese Month (May 5 - June 4), the 7th Chinese Month (August 7 - September 6), and the 10th Chinese Month (November 7 - December 6). You should be careful of accidents from sharp metal tools and machinery. Be careful of arguments with your neighbors. Also, be careful of disputes that may lead to lawsuits. Also, be careful of losing valuables, being stolen, or being harmed by criminals. Take care of your family members and be careful of accidents during work. Also, do not get involved in conflicts between your friends. Be careful of some friends betraying you harassing you and slandering you Or physical harm.

Love

For the seniors, this year you should try not to interfere or be fussy with your children's affairs. You will be respected and loved by them as usual. For young people, this year is considered a year of strong charm. You will receive attention from many people of the opposite sex. However, please do not be hasty. You should date thoroughly and maintain your attitude first. Wait until you are sure before taking the relationship to the next level. It is not too late. Because at your age, you still have a lot of time to get to know each other. Do not expect to date only superficially and charm the other person. Causing the other person to misunderstand will create bad karma and make the love unfulfilled. In addition, you must know how to control yourself, especially during the 1st Chinese Month (February 3 – March 4), the 4th Chinese Month (May 5 – June 4), the 7th Chinese Month (August 7 – September 6), and the 10th Chinese Month (November 7 – December 6), when you must be careful not to let the atmosphere take over you. It may cause damage later. Do not forget the old saying that says do not be too hasty because if anything happens, you will lose your future. And be careful not to get involved in your friends' love affairs. And you should avoid going to entertainment venues, which will only bring bad luck.

Health

For seniors, this year, health is not so good. Old illnesses often show annoying symptoms. Therefore, you should get enough rest. Take care of eating food that is easy to digest and nutritious to build immunity against illnesses. This will save you money on medical treatment. Especially during the 1st Chinese month (February 3 - March 4), the 4th Chinese month (May 5 - June 4), the 7th Chinese month (August 7 - September 6), and the 10th Chinese month (November 7 - December 6), be careful of aches and pains, bone pain, or fainting, which may cause you to slip and fall, which can be dangerous. Therefore, you should not go to strange places. When leaving the house, seniors should have someone to take care of them. In addition, you must be careful of diabetes or heart disease. For young people, be careful of allergies, and infectious diseases caused by eating whatever you like. Be careful of accidents while traveling, both near and far.

Year of the MONKEY (Fire) | (1956) & (2016)

" The MONKEY on the mountain" is a person born in the year of the MONKEY at the age of 69 years (1956) and 9 years (2016)

Overview

For senior horoscopes in this age group, this year is a good time for investment. It is suitable to choose a close heir to take over the work, to train as a representative to lighten your burden. The horoscope owner should change his role to be behind the scenes, step down from work, and take more time to rest. This year, the overall direction of work and trade is still considered to grow quite well, but it will be slow and gradual. There are still channels for making money from investments during the year, but during the year, there will be a group of bad stars that will affect you in many ways. The first is health problems. Be careful of stomach problems, intestinal diseases, and infectious diseases. You must also be more careful of accidents both while working and traveling. You may injure your legs. The second is arguments. When you see something, it seems unpleasant, and you cannot help but tell them off. You have to accept this. The best thing to do is not to get involved in other people's problems and not to criticize your children or grandchildren. Let go of some things because good intentions sometimes make you stressed out. The third is losing your wealth, whether it is from damaged or lost valuables or being a victim of fraud. Because this year is considered one of the unlucky zodiac signs, at the beginning of the year, the person with the horoscope should find time to pay homage to the Tai Sui deity to ward off bad luck. It will help protect the person with the horoscope to be happy and healthy, free from illness and danger.

For young people, this year, they should be careful of some friends who invite them to hang out or play games outside the house. If it is too much, it will be bad for both their studies and health. In addition, they should be careful while playing sports or doing activities outside because they may get injured and lose their property. At the beginning of the year, parents should take their children to pay homage to the Tai Sui deity to ask for his blessing to protect them from bad luck and danger.

Career and Business

This year, the career of the person will experience a storm because the horoscope has a group of bad stars aiming at them, which often results in conflicts. In addition, problems with customers or people you have to do business with can easily occur. You should also be careful about bad debts or problems with government agencies or the Revenue Department, especially during the months when the career star is low. There will be unexpected obstacles and work will be hindered, such as the 1st Chinese month (February 3 - March 4), the 4th Chinese month (May 5 - June 4), the 7th Chinese month (August 7 - September 6), and the 10th Chinese month (November 7 - December 6). You must be careful about signing contracts and documents. Do not be greedy for advice from people close to you. Instead, you should carefully examine the details of the contract to avoid problems

later. This year, when starting a new job, entering into a joint venture, or investing, you should analyze carefully before investing.
Do not be fooled by sweet words or believe in persuasion easily. There is a chance of damage or injury. Also, be careful of conflicts in the organization that will cause damage to work and accounting fraud.

For the child horoscope person This year you should be more diligent and pay more attention to your lessons. Don't get addicted to games or be too concerned with playing. If you have true determination, you will make much progress this year. The good months for both work and study for this person in both age cycles are the 2nd Chinese month (March 5 - April 3), the 3rd Chinese month (April 4 - May 4), the 5th Chinese month (June 5 - July 6), and the 9th Chinese month (October 8 - November 6).

Financial

This year, your finances are in a state of losing money. At the beginning of the year, you may solve the problem by buying expensive items that you like to reduce the power of sucking money out of your pocket. In particular, you should be careful during the following months when your finances will easily leak out and you should plan your finances and investments carefully, namely, the 1st Chinese month (February 3 – March 4), the 4th Chinese month (May 5 – June 4), the 7th Chinese month (August 7 – September 6), and the 10th Chinese month (November 7 – December 6). You must be careful of current expenses that will reduce your liquidity and cause you to lose money. Also, you must not gamble, borrow money from close friends sign as financial guarantors, and invest in illegal businesses. The months when your finances are smooth and flowing well are the 2nd Chinese month (March 5 – April 3), the 3rd Chinese month (April 4 – May 4), the 5th Chinese month (June 5 – July 6), and the 9th Chinese month (October 8 – November 6).

Family

This year, your family horoscope is not very good. There will be conflicts with people in the house. For the elders, be careful with your words that may make the children lose their respect. Therefore, you should act as a consultant, give advice, and give blessings when they come to you. Do not let your emotions take over and avoid interfering with your children's matters, especially during the following months: 1st Chinese month (February 3 – March 4), the 4th Chinese month (May 5 – June 4), the 7th Chinese month (August 7 – September 6), the 10th Chinese month (November 7 – December 6). In addition, you must be careful of family members or subordinates making small problems into big problems. Be careful of losing valuables, being stolen, or falling victim to criminals.

Love

This year, love is not smooth. It is easy to take your emotions out on others. Therefore, even though you are a couple who have been together until old age and the promotion period is over, you can still say that you have shared both happiness and sorrow for a long time. You should continue to take care of and cherish each other's feelings, especially during the months when love is fragile and easily leads to arguments, such as the 1st Chinese month (February 3 - March 4), the 4th Chinese month (May 5 - June 4), the 7th Chinese month (August 7 - September 6), and the 10th Chinese month (November 7 - December 6). You should try to control your emotions well, avoid triggers that lead to arguments, and avoid going to entertainment venues, massage parlors, and others.

Health

This year, the health of the person will not be smooth, especially the elderly who will have both old and new illnesses, including the common symptoms of back pain, toothache, waist pain, and knee pain. Be careful of accidents that may cause injury. And there is something to be concerned about, which is being careful of hidden illnesses. Therefore, you should observe for any abnormal symptoms in your body, such as feeling a lump or any organs that are swollen or have lymph fluid. You should see a doctor for a detailed examination. Especially the unsupportive months and you must be especially careful about your health are the 1st Chinese month (February 3 - March 4), the 4th Chinese month (May 5 - June 4), the 7th Chinese month (August 7 - September 6), and the 10th Chinese month (November 7 - December 6). You should be more careful of accidents, especially dangers from driving and traveling. You should get enough rest and be strict about eating nutritious food and should not interfere in other people's business. Letting go will help you feel at ease. For children, be careful of the dangers of unclean food that may cause diarrhea or other infectious diseases, and accidents while playing and doing outdoor activities.

Year of the MONKEY (Earth) | (1968)

" The Monkey Love in the Freedom " is a person born in the year of the MONKEY at the age of 57 years (1968)

Overview

The horoscope for this age group, since this year is another year that will receive the clashing power (in a bad way) from Tai Sui (the god who protects the horoscope of the year), this year many activities of the horoscope must be considered before doing. Because the horoscope house is facing an inauspicious constellation, which will affect the work and trade. There are often problems in personnel management that will cause conflicts within the organization. In terms of business and trade, there will be fluctuations from external factors that are beyond our control. In terms of finances, be careful of problems with bad debt accounts. Work will show mistakes and damages from unclear communication or production of products that are out of fashion or being bullied and pushed out of the way. In addition, you should be careful of unexpected events that may happen to family members. Accidents from electrical appliances or steel frames, roof frames, or other equipment that are high up. You must check the safety conditions often. If there is any damage or weakness, you should repair it immediately. Do not let it fall and harm people in the house. Including health problems of the horoscope, including using the road, do not be careless or hasty. This year, at the beginning of the year, you should find time to pay respect to Tai Sui. To ward off misfortune and improve one's destiny to live happily, to make a living, and to be safe from all kinds of bad things and dangers.

Career and Business

This year, your work will encounter storms. You will have to work two or three times harder to get what you need. You must also be careful of conflicts within your organization or department, work postponements, or incidents that may cause damage or disruption to your work. In addition, you must be careful of subordinates or servants who are dishonest or cause damage to your department. Those who do business should be careful of disputes with customers or business partners, which may be caused by counterfeit or substandard products. In particular, the months when your work will encounter obstacles and problems, including business, are the 1st Chinese month (February 3 – March 4), the 4th Chinese month (May 5 – June 4), the 7th Chinese month (August 7 – September 6), and the 10th Chinese month (November 7 – December 6). You should be more careful and prepare for changes that may occur. Avoid being quick-tempered and emotional, so as not to make problems worse. Be careful when signing employment contracts or accepting work, including any legal transactions that have long-term binding effects. You must be even more careful. Joint ventures and investments during these months tend to have negative effects. There is a high chance of being deceived or suffering damages. Therefore, please do not fall for sweet words of flattery to get you to invest. You will encounter problems later. The months when your work and investments will be bright and prosperous are the 2nd Chinese month (March 5– April 3), the 3rd Chinese month (April 4 – May 4), the 5th Chinese month (June 5 – July 6), and the 9th Chinese month (October 8 – November 6).

Financial

This year, the owner's finances are satisfactory. Direct income from salary and trade will have enough income to circulate and spend continuously. However, in terms of luck from gambling, you cannot expect it to be a life-or-death situation because you may get hurt. You should not be greedy for luck that is not yours and should be careful of unexpected current expenses that may drain your liquidity. In particular, the months when your finances will be stuck are the 1st Chinese month (February 3 - March 4), the 4th Chinese month (May 5 - June 4), the 7th Chinese month (August 7 - September 6), and the 10th Chinese month (November 7 - December 6). You should not gamble. Do not lend money or sign as a guarantee. Do not invest in businesses that are likely to be illegal or immoral. The bad karma will catch up to you quickly. The months when your finances will return to being smooth and flexible are the 2nd Chinese month (March 5–April 3), the 3rd Chinese month (April 4 – May 4), the 5th Chinese month (June 5 – July 6), and the 9th Chinese month (October 8 – November 6).

Family

This year, the important thing in your family is to be careful of accidents or unexpected events. Be careful of close friends who do not wish you well, who will betray you, slander you, or even harm you. In particular, during the months when you need to be careful of conflicts and unrest in your home, namely the 1st Chinese month (February 3 – March 4), the 4th Chinese month (May 5 – June 4), the 7th Chinese month (August 7 – September 6), and the 10th Chinese month (November 7 – December 6), you need to be especially careful of safety and accidents in your home. Be careful of losing valuables, being stolen, or falling victim to scammers. Try to avoid triggers that will cause conflict in your family. Be careful of subordinates or servants who cause trouble and damage. Be careful of people in your home arguing with your neighbors. In addition, avoid traveling to isolated places, stay away from untrustworthy friends, and do not get involved in other people's conflicts.

Love

This year, even though your love horoscope is moderate, there will often be reasons for you and your lover to be suspicious of each other. Therefore, you must not be easily influenced and must not let work take over you until you have no time for your family or lover. It would be better if you find time to eat together or go on vacation together and be firm to break down the wall of misunderstanding. In particular, during the months when your love is rather fragile, you will encounter disagreements and easily have arguments, namely, the 1st Chinese month (February 3 – March 4), the 4th Chinese month (May 5 – June 4), the 7th Chinese month (August 7 – September 6), and the 10th Chinese month (November 7 – December 6). During these periods, learn to control your emotions and not let menopause hormones destroy a good relationship. Also, avoid going to various types of entertainment venues. Also, do not get involved in other people's families.

Health

Your health is not good. You should be careful of high blood pressure, liver disease, and heart disease. Therefore, you should take care of yourself by finding enough time to rest and doing light exercises that are appropriate for your age. The months in which you should take special care of your health are the 1st Chinese month (February 3 - March 4), the 4th Chinese month (May 5 - June 4), the 7th Chinese month (August 7 - September 6), and the 10th Chinese month (November 7 - December 6) when your health is not so good. You should be careful of fatigue, dizziness, road accidents, and accidents during work. Be careful of diseases spreading and erupting, especially for those with chronic diseases. In addition, you should avoid alcoholic beverages and e-cigarettes.

Year of the MONKEY (Wood) | (1980)

" The Monkey eats fruit" is a person born in the year of the MONKEY at the age of 45 years (1980)

Overview

For the person born in the year of the Rooster, this year, many things will be smoothed out for you. Although your birth year is another year that receives the power of the Tai Sui deity (the deity who protects your destiny) which is the power of hatred and harm, because the auspicious star in the zodiac sign shines and supports you, if you are steadfast in your goodness, diligent in your work without giving up, and constantly develop your skills and add new knowledge to yourself without stopping, then your career or business will progress. And even though you are surrounded by pressure and obstacles in many areas, there are opportunities for you to overcome them. There are opportunities to build yourself up, expand your work, increase your production, create work, or expand your income, all of which have the opportunity to receive good feedback. But what you should be especially careful about this year is health problems, family member safety, problems with illnesses such as high blood pressure, cerebrovascular disease, high cholesterol, or head injuries. Or the person often has frequent headaches. In addition, you must be more careful in your life. Do not be careless with accidents both while working and using the road. Another thing you should be careful about is that investing this year will be very risky. Therefore, you should study and find information carefully. Also, you should not get involved in other people's matters. Because there may be a side effect of having to suffer misfortune from something you did not do. And you should be careful not to fall victim to fraudsters. At the beginning of the year, you should find time to pay homage to the Tai Sui deity to ask for his protection to ward off misfortune and ask for blessings to help your work and business go smoothly.

Career and Business

This year, since many auspicious stars are moving in the zodiac, it will help promote your career and business to flourish. If you have planned and prepared something and have not succeeded, please check your readiness. If the factors in many aspects are in place, this year will be a good time for you to start a new job. Start small and gradually develop. You can go all out because your career and business will have opportunities to progress well, especially during the 2nd Chinese month (March 5 – April 3), 3rd Chinese month (April 4 – May 4), 5th Chinese month (June 5 – July 6) and 9th Chinese month (October 8 – November 6). However, you should be careful during the months when your work will make mistakes and damages. You should not invest with only a positive perspective. Be careful of hidden corners that you do not expect. You should also be more careful when performing legal contracts. In particular, the months when work will experience problems and obstacles are the 1st Chinese month (February 3 - March 4), the 4th Chinese month (May 5 - June 4), the 7th Chinese month (August 7 - September 6), and the 10th Chinese month (November 7 - December 6). During these times, you should avoid investing because you are likely to be deceived. Beware of insider accounting fraud. Beware of external economic fluctuations and unexpected changes.

Financial

This year, your finances will be in the opposite direction of your career, as expenses will be queuing up to catch up with your income. There will also be unexpected losses of large sums of money. Therefore, you should save anything you can. Do not spend lavishly on trivial matters. Do not lend money to anyone or be a guarantor for someone close to you. You should also not gamble or take risks. Do not do risky businesses or businesses that violate the law, as you may be fined and cannot escape prosecution. In particular, the months that are not favorable to you are the 1st Chinese month (3 February 3 – 4 March 4), the 4th Chinese month (5 May 5 – 4 June 4), the 7th Chinese month (7 August 7 – 6 September 6), and the 10th Chinese month (7 November 7 – 6 December 6). The months in which your financial luck flows smoothly are the 2nd

Chinese month (March 5 – April 3), the 3rd Chinese month (April 4 – May 4), the 5th Chinese month (June 5 – July 6), and the 9th Chinese month (October 8 – November 6).

Family

This year, the family of this person will have auspicious power. At home, there will be a patron and an opportunity to buy expensive property. There will be an auspicious time to move into a new house. If this year your family has an opportunity to organize an auspicious event, it will help reduce the clashing power of the year. However, you should be careful during the months when there will be problems and arguments within the family, which are the 1st Chinese month (February 3 - March 4), the 4th Chinese month (May 5 - June 4), the 7th Chinese month (August 7 - September 6), and the 10th Chinese month (November 7 - December 6).

You must be especially careful of accidents in the house. Electrical appliances, gas stoves, or other flame-generating items must be taken care of to prevent any bad things from happening. Valuables must be stored neatly and securely because there may be a thief breaking into the house.

In addition, you must be on the lookout for the dangers of falling victim to scammers in the house. You should not get involved in conflicts between friends. Be careful of friends who will betray you or find a way to harass, slander, harm you, or find a reason to destroy your reputation.

Love

This year, your love life is quite smooth. If you are single, someone of the opposite sex will come to take care of you. For those who have a lover or partner, your lover will be very considerate and understanding. This year is suitable for taking your lover on a vacation. It will help you feel refreshed and cheerful. Taking each other to the temple to make merit will help improve your love life even more. However, during this year, due to the power of the Peach Blossom, be careful of infatuation or misbehavior that will turn small things into big problems. Especially during the 1st Chinese Month (February 3 - March 4), the 4th Chinese Month (May 5 - June 4), the 7th Chinese Month (August 7 - September 6), and the 10th Chinese Month (November 7 - December 6), the person should be firm. Please remember that temporary happiness can bring endless trouble and chaos to the family. Also, please refrain from getting involved in other people's families. You should not go to entertainment venues.

Health

The health horoscope is not very good. It is because of the influence of the Tai Sui god's Chong energy affecting health problems, especially heart disease, stomach disease, intestinal disease, localized pain, and beware of accidents. Especially during the months when your health horoscope will have complications or old diseases will flare up, namely, the 1st Chinese month (February 3 - March 4), the 4th Chinese month (May 5 - June 4), the 7th Chinese month (August 7 - September 6), and the 10th Chinese month (November 7 - December 6). Be more careful about taking care of your health, avoid eating cold foods, beware of allergies, and beware of injuries from using the road.

Year of the MONKEY (Golden) | (1992)

" The monkey is smart." is a person born in the year of the MONKEY at the age of 33 years (1992)

Overview

For the Monkey in this age group, this year, the career of the Monkey will have a path of progress and prosperity. The work will catch the eyes of the elders and there will be an opportunity for you to show your abilities and learn to improve and change your work, analyze your strengths and weaknesses, as well as the opportunities in your work, and use them to your advantage. Therefore, this year is considered a year of good opportunities. The Monkey should be diligent and determined to create work. You must also diligently add new skills and knowledge to yourself to keep up with external changes. Then you will have a bright future and be able to improve your quality of life. However, you must be careful because your work may be envied by some people. Therefore, if you do not know how to be humble, and control your emotions and words, you are likely to be bullied and slandered. This is because the Monkey sign is another sign that receives the power of the Tai Sui god, which is the power of hatred and slander. In addition, during the year, there will be many bad stars that will harass your horoscope house, which will affect your life in many ways. The first is work and finances. Although there are many smooth periods suitable for increasing work, expanding sales, expanding production, and increasing investment, there are many periods when unexpected expenses will appear and drain your liquidity. Therefore, you should be careful when investing. The secondary problem is health problems, even though you are still at an age full of energy. But knowing how to compromise in life is also essential. You should set aside time for adequate rest, use your free time to exercise to build up your health, choose nutritious foods, and be careful after drinking and driving because it can be dangerous. The Monkey Year in the Snake Year 2025 is considered to be another unlucky zodiac sign. Therefore, at the beginning of the year, you should find an opportunity to pay respect to Tai Sui to ask for blessings and eliminate bad luck, to help your life be safe, happy, and smooth.

Career and Business

This year, the career and trade of the person must be careful under the unstable variables and some things are beyond control. If you are not too impatient, there is still room for advancement. However, if you are going to travel this way, you should create alliances to support you to overcome this. The meaning is to constantly create and strengthen good relationships with people around you and outsiders that you have to contact all the time. Therefore, there will be an opportunity to create good results. Especially during the months when your career and trade have a positive direction, namely, the 2nd Chinese month (March 5 - April 3), the 3rd Chinese month (April 4 - May 4), the 5th Chinese month (June 5 - July 6), and the 9th Chinese month (October 8 - November 6). Various investments still have investment channels that can create good returns. However, you should be careful during the months when your work will be stuck and have obstacles and problems, namely the 1st Chinese month (February 3 – March 4), the 4th Chinese month (May 5 – June 4), the 7th Chinese month (August 7 – September 6), and the 10th Chinese month (November 7 – December 6). Do not invest during these periods because you may get hurt or lose your job. You should communicate clearly in your work to avoid any damage. You should also be careful of people with ill intentions who plan to harass you to eliminate you from the path and cause your work to reach a critical point.

Financial

This year's finances are a guideline for caution. Both income and expenses are often fluctuating and difficult to control. Therefore, spending frugally is the primary solution. In addition, be careful of unexpected expenses, especially during the months when your finances will be low and sluggish, and you should plan carefully, which are the 1st Chinese month (February 3 – March 4), the 4th Chinese month (May 5 – June 4), the 7th Chinese month (August 7 – September 6), and the 10th Chinese month (November 7 – December 6). Gambling is prohibited. Lending money or signing financial guarantees is prohibited. Investment in illegal or immoral businesses is prohibited. The months when your finances will flow smoothly are the 2nd Chinese month (March 5 – April 3), the 3rd Chinese month (April 4 – May 4), the 5th Chinese month (June 5 – July 6), and the 9th Chinese month (October 8 – November 6).

Family

This year, your family will lack peace. There may be arguments, conflicts, and health problems of the elderly. People in the house may get sick. Be careful of losing valuables or being stolen. In addition, be careful of people in the house falling victim to scammers. You should not get involved or interfere in your friends' conflicts. You should stay away from friends who want to take advantage of you. In particular, there are months when conflicts or problems in your family are likely to easily occur: 1st Chinese month (February 3 – March 4), 4th Chinese month (May 5 – June 4), 7th Chinese month (August 7 – September 6), and 10th Chinese month (November 7 – December 6). You must be careful of unexpected events that may cause injuries to people in the house. Be careful of servants or subordinates causing trouble.

Love

This year, the love horoscope of the person is good. Those who are single have a chance to succeed in love. Those who have a lover or partner will receive more attention, help, sharing, and sympathy because you will have the opportunity to travel with your lover or partner to be comfortable. This will allow you to talk to and understand each other in the obstacles. However, during the 1st Chinese month (February 3 - March 4), the 4th Chinese month (May 5 - June 4), the 7th Chinese month (August 7 - September 6), and the 10th Chinese month (November 7 - December 6), the person must avoid going to social gatherings at entertainment venues because it will cause arguments and chaos. Also, be careful not to get involved in other people's families. This will cause bad karma and bring endless trouble.

Health

This year, the health of the person is not very good. Be careful of gastritis and intestinal diseases. Take care of your drinking and eating hygiene. In addition, you should eat on time. If you do not have time to eat, drink milk from a box or hot Ovaltine. You should not drink or eat cold things such as ice or things that are too cold. You should also be careful of injuries to your head or legs. In particular, the months that you should be especially careful are the 1st Chinese month (February 3 - March 4), the 4th Chinese month (May 5 - June 4), the 7th Chinese month (August 7 - September 6), and the 10th Chinese month (November 7 - December 6). You should be more careful of accidents both while working and traveling. In addition, observe for pain or soreness in specific areas. If you find any, you should see a doctor immediately to find the cause. You should not buy medicine to take by yourself frequently.

Chinese Astrology Horoscope for Each Month

Month 12 in the Dragon Year (5 Jan 25 - 2 Feb 25)

Your horoscope for those born in the Year of the Monkey, at the beginning of the Chinese New Year this month, will encounter obstacles. Many activities and work will not go as smoothly as you wish. You should not be hasty in thinking or doing anything during this period because mistakes and damages can easily occur. What you should do this month is to summarize the financial figures from the past year to make the direction clearer. During this time, you should prepare to evaluate your potential in various aspects, both strengths and weaknesses, things that made profits and things that lost must be cut out. Think of ways to solve problems for the parts that are still lacking.

In addition, you should be careful not to leak important information because it could be a threat to yourself in the future. Fortunately, in terms of work, you are in a position where you do a lot and earn a lot. Therefore, you must increase your diligence, never stop learning and developing yourself, aim to find new opportunities to create work, expand sales and income, and diligently save money for emergencies so that you do not have to run around looking for money. In terms of investment, there are some periods when it is possible to invest, but you should study all aspects of the information carefully.

Although your financial fortune this month has enough income, you should spend it sparingly and only use what is necessary. There is still a chance to gamble and take risks this month, but please do not spend too much.

In terms of family, there is peace. Love is not so good. Misunderstandings often occur, leading to arguments. Therefore, you should avoid going to entertainment venues and spend more time with your lover, which will help reduce problems. For relatives, be careful of being tricked or causing trouble, so you should keep your distance.

Health-wise, even though you are quite strong, you should be careful of accidents from driving, especially after a party. You should avoid driving.

Support Days: 3 Jan., 7 Jan., 11 Jan., 15 Jan., 19 Jan., 23 Jan., 27 Jan., 31 Jan.
Lucky Days: 12 Jan., 24 Jan.
Misfortune Days: 9 Jan., 21 Jan.
Bad Days: 6 Jan.,18 Jan., 30 Jan.

Month 1 in the Snake Year (3 Feb 25 – 4 Mar 25)
This month, your fortune is still declining. At the beginning of the year, you should find an opportunity to worship Tai Sui to ward off bad luck. Also, make merit and worship Buddha in various places to bring good fortune to you and your family. Then, you should set goals for your work and life, prepare a budget for income and expenses that you need to use in your business and family and allocate it well while the money is still flowing smoothly so that you have some left over for savings.

In terms of work, you will encounter obstacles. There will be conflicts and chaos both internally and externally. You should frequently contact those you need to contact with a friendly attitude to help improve many things.

In addition, when signing documents, contracts, or legal transactions that are binding, you should read them carefully. Do not be hasty, so that you will not have any worries later. Starting a new job or making investments is not a good time. You should wait a bit longer.

For your salary, your income will be low while your expenses will be high. If possible, you should make a financial plan to allocate a budget for various activities. You should also not invest in risky businesses or gamble. Do not lend money or sign financial guarantees. You should not be greedy for ill-gotten gains. You should also regularly check your accounts.

A peaceful and smooth family In terms of close friends and relatives, during this period, speak only as little as necessary. Speaking too much may bring disaster to yourself.

In terms of love, you will encounter waves and winds. Avoid going to entertainment venues because you may encounter more disasters and suffering.

In terms of physical health, during this period, you will often have headaches. You should get enough sleep. Also, be careful of injuries to your hands and legs.

Support Days: 4 Feb., 8 Feb., 12 Feb., 16 Feb., 20 Feb., 24 Feb., 28 Feb.
Lucky Days: 5 Feb., 17 Feb.
Misfortune Days: 2 Feb., 14 Feb., 26 Feb.
Bad Days: 11 Feb., 23 Feb.

Month 2 in the Snake Year (5 Mar 25 - 3 Apr 25)
This month, your horoscope has overcome the power of conflict. The life graph of the Monkey Year people is on the rise, causing many obstacles and problems to ease. Your work and

business will receive help, causing changes in a better direction. Therefore, what you should do during this period is to prepare to create more work and increase sales. You should go all out to have support channels. The more you do, the more chances you will receive money. Importantly, the work you do must be of quality. Do not only aim for profit. You must use your relationship skills and close friendships to expand the market.

In terms of work, you must be diligent. There will be progress as a reward. Know your enemy and yourself. Keep studying and adding new skills and things to your work. Like this, no matter what the fight is, it will not be defeated. Collaboration, investing, or investing in various areas is good during this period.

This month, your financial horoscope is prosperous, both direct income and special income. You will also receive windfall luck because you have many ways to make money, resulting in a large income. However, when you have money, you should manage and allocate it well, dividing one part for spending, another part for saving, and another part for investment.

As for the family situation, this month is peaceful and smooth. As for relatives and friends, you will find someone to help with the work. And rely on both work and financial assistance.

Health-wise, you will experience illness. See a doctor for treatment. Regular exercise will help you stay healthy and have immunity to illness.

Love this month is paved with rose petals. For those whose hearts are still empty, you will meet someone you like who you have been waiting for.

Support Days: 4 Mar, 8 Mar., 12 Mar., 16 Mar., 20 Mar., 24 Mar., 28 Mar.
Lucky Days: 1 Mar, 13 Mar., 25 Mar..
Misfortune Days: 10 Mar, 22 Mar., 12 Mar.
Bad Days: 7 Mar, 19 Mar., 31 Mar.

Month 3 in the Snake Year (4 Apr 25 - 4 May 25)
This month, the horoscope of those born in the year of the Monkey moves to meet the friendly line. In addition, there will be a shining auspicious star, which will help your work and business to go smoothly. What you should do this month, in addition to pioneering to expand your work and branches, and continuously increase your sales and income, you should also prepare to organize your internal management system, whether it is rotating personnel work, arranging people to be suitable for the work, or improving some work to support technology, so as not to lose good opportunities that come your way. In addition, in terms of personal matters, you should not neglect to adjust yourself to people at both the upper level, which is your supervisor, and colleagues, and the lower level, which is your subordinates, to strengthen good relationships that will facilitate smoothness in your work.

This month's finances are quite good. Cash flow will flow in from things you have invested and worked hard on before, including your current work. As for working together, starting a new job, investing in shares, and investing in various channels, this is a good time when obstacles stop, so you can proceed.

This month, your family horoscope is still smooth and normal. Your health is quite good, but you still have to be careful of accidents while traveling both near and far. After a party, if you have been drinking alcohol, you should avoid driving.

In terms of love, it is time to make a decision. If you want to ask, go ask quickly, don't wait until next year, otherwise someone else will take it and eat it.

Support Days: 1 Apr., 5 Apr., 9 Apr., 13 Apr., 17 Apr., 21 Apr., 25 Apr., 29 Apr.
Lucky Days: 6 Apr., 18 Apr., 30 Apr.
Misfortune Days: 3 Apr., 15 Apr., 27 Apr.
Bad Days: 12 Apr., 24 Apr.

Month 4 in the Snake Year (5 May 25 - 4 Jun 25)

This month, your horoscope will encounter an inauspicious star orbiting to disturb you. Things that were going well will become unsmooth. On the contrary, they will cause damage to you. Your work and business during this period may not go as smoothly as you hoped. On this occasion, you should be careful of your temper. Even if your work starts to have problems, do not take it out on others to reduce the obstacles that will come back and the lack of cooperation in your department. Therefore, you must know how to control your temper. Do not act without thinking. This month, there are still ways to make money. Please maintain your perseverance. You should also take good care of your work and not interfere with others' work. In terms of starting a new job, investing in shares, and various investments, there is a chance of being cheated. Do not listen to sweet words.

This month, your finances will be in a state of losing money. Therefore, you should be careful that your liquidity will be interrupted. Do not lend money or accept guarantees. Do not gamble and take risks. Do not get involved in counterfeit or illegal products.

This month, your family will be peaceful and have auspicious energy entering the house. Regarding relatives, there is a lack of good. Be careful of being slandered, betrayed, or secretly attacked because of words that may offend someone. Therefore, during this time, you should keep your mouth shut.

In terms of love, this is the time when the love tree of a relationship will blossom and bear fruit. The relationship will grow comfortably.

In terms of health, it is not very good. Be strict about your diet and take care of getting enough sleep. Do not be careless with accidents while using the road.

Support Days: 3 May, 7 May, 11 May, 15 May, 19 May, 23 May, 27 May, 31 May.
Lucky Days: 12 May, 24 May
Misfortune Days: 9 May, 21 May.

Bad Days: 6 May, 18 May, 30 May

Month 5 in the Snake Year (5 Jun 25 - 6 Jul 25)
This month, your life path will improve, but internal problems and obstacles remain. During this time, what you should do is ask for advice from those who have experience in solving problems. In addition, you must be honest and determined in your work. Always add new skills to yourself. This will help you to be aware of many work obstacles and solve them better. The important thing is not to be discouraged or not to change anything. Take care of the original responsibility. Do it slowly and save it.

In addition, you must try to solve conflicts at work. Save money and wait for a good time to move forward with full power. As for investment, you still need to consider carefully before doing anything.

This month, your finances are balanced, so you have some money left, even if it is not much. However, you should set aside some for emergency savings. Do not lend money to others or be a guarantor.

During this time, your family horoscope, even though you have found a sponsor, you still need to increase security measures at home and for the health of the elderly because there will be problems that cause you to lose money from medical expenses.

In terms of physical health, you still need to take care of your drinking and eating habits. Be careful of food poisoning, pain in specific areas, infectious diseases, and injuries from accidents both while working and traveling.

As for love, even though you may disagree with each other, please be patient. Do not use your emotions to spite each other or find reasons to taunt the other person. You should also avoid visiting entertainment venues.

Support Days: 4 Jun., 8 Jun., 12 Jun., 16 Jun., 20 Jun., 24 Jun., 28 Jun.
Lucky Days: 5 Jun., 17 Jun., 29 Jun.

Misfortune Days: 2 Jun., 14 Jun., 26 Jun.
Bad Days: 11 Jun., 23 Jun.

Month 6 in the Snake Year (7 Jul 25 - 7 Aug 25)

This month, the horoscope of those born in the year of the Monkey is in a downward trend. Your career and business must be managed carefully because there is a chance of unexpected events.

What you should do during this period is to learn to know the word "patience" and learn to "put yourself in other people's shoes". Don't just be selfish and not consider others. It will be difficult to be together like this. In terms of work, this period will face storms because there will be unexpected changes. If you are still a dinosaur, there is a chance of being eliminated. Therefore, you should use your skills to quickly improve and change in time to catch up with them.

This month, even though your income is steady and normal, you still have to strictly control your spending. You must also be careful not to be deceived by scammers.

When thinking of investing in any area, you must study and consider carefully. Do not be greedy and fall into the trap of others. It will cause you to lose a large sum of money.
In addition, you should be careful when signing contracts that may have hidden clauses that take advantage of you. You should read and ask questions carefully. Investments are not good. There is a chance that you will be deceived and damaged.

There will still be things within the family that will cause you to be troubled and unhappy this month. Be careful of people in the house getting injured from using tools and machinery, and be careful of thieves.

Health is not so good. Be careful of stomach diseases, intestinal diseases, and accidents while traveling.

Love is not good this month. An unstable and easily irritated mind makes it easy to have arguments.

Support Days: 2 Jul., 6 Jul., 10 Jul., 14 Jul., 18 Jul., 22 Jul., 26 Jul., 30 Jul.
Lucky Days: 11 Jul., 23 Jul.
Misfortune Days: 8 Jul., 20 Jul.
Bad Days: 5 Jul., 17 Jul., 29 Jul.

Month 7 in the Snake Year (8 Aug 25 - 7 Sep 25)
This month, the horoscope of those born in the year of the Monkey is moving to encounter obstacles, so unusual things often happen. Your work and business will face many obstacles, all of which are challenges that test your abilities. Therefore, what you should do during this period is to see clearly before doing any activities. You cannot be impatient or let your emotions take over.

In addition, you must know how to adjust yourself to the situation with obstacles. You must find ways to expand your income and delay payments to maintain liquidity in the system.

In terms of work, bad stars are harassing you. Therefore, during this period, you must be careful not to make mistakes or cause damage, because you may lose your job or not receive any work. You should also be careful of internal conflicts that will hinder you, causing problems in your work.

This month, your financial horoscope is not good because there will be financial leakages. Therefore, you must be careful of corruption and unexpected losses. In addition, you should not gamble.

You should not be involved in anything illegal. Do not create long-term debts. Be careful of customer accounts that may go bankrupt. You should refrain from investing during this period.

For your family, this month is still not smooth. You must be careful of arguments due to disagreements. It is better to try to speak calmly and avoid prolonging things. You should also be careful of the elderly or servants in the house causing trouble. Relatives will meet friends who want to gain benefits.

Love this month will be sweet and you will understand each other well. However, you must be careful about your health, you may get stomach problems, intestinal problems, headaches, and dizziness. You must also be careful of dangers while traveling, which may cause injuries.

Support Days: 3 Aug., 7 Aug., 11 Aug., 15 Aug., 19 Aug., 23 Aug., 27 Aug., 31 Aug.
Lucky Days: 4 Aug., 16 Aug., 28 Aug.
Misfortune Days: 1 Aug., 13 Aug., 25 Aug.
Bad Days: 10 Aug., 22 Aug.

Month 8 in the Snake Year (7 Sep 25 - 7 Oct 25)

This month, your fate has auspicious stars gathering and shining brightly, causing those who are stuck and difficult to find helpers. This is the opportunity to do so, which is to clear up the backlog of work and solve the problems you have in the past, to prepare for creating work and making more sales. In addition, you should always build and strengthen good relationships with people around you, to reduce obstacles and receive support and assistance.

In terms of work, during this period, you must be responsible. When you promise to do something, you should do it successfully. Do not abandon the work halfway. In addition, there is a risk of being cheated when signing a contract to accept work or hire someone.

For this salary, the more you do, the more you get paid, so you should be diligent so that the money will grow. In addition, investing in gold will give good and interesting returns. As for investments this month, the direction is bright, there will be a way to make money.

In terms of family, you will find auspicious energy visiting. In the house, there is a chance to organize an auspicious event, whether it is a birthday celebration, a housewarming party, a graduation party, or an opportunity to welcome and congratulate a new little member of the family. Some people may have a chance to move into a new house or workplace. Relatives and friends who have problems will receive good cooperation and help, and during this time you may receive useful advice for your work.

Love is sweet, take care of each other and remember all the good events so that in the future if there is a problem, you will be able to think of this bright day.

Support Days: 1 Sep, 5 Sep., 9 Sep, 13 Sep, 17 Sep., 21 Sep., 25 Sep., 29 Sep.
Lucky Days: 9 Sep, 21 Sep
Misfortune Days: 6 Sep, 18 Sep, 30 Sep
Bad Days: 3 Sep, 15 Sep, 27 Sep

Month 9 in the Snake Year (8 Oct 25 - 6 Nov 25)
This month, those born in the year of the Monkey will receive auspicious power from the auspicious stars that will shine to help. Their careers and businesses will therefore find a path of continuous prosperity. This is because this period of work and business is a golden opportunity to show their abilities. There will also be many channels open for you to turn

your work into money. For those who have regular jobs, there is a chance that you will be considered for a promotion. Therefore, what should not be overlooked during this period is to build and strengthen good relationships with people you have to contact. This will help expand your career base and give you more bargaining power. Any contact, negotiation, or coordination during this period will therefore go smoothly like peeling a banana.

This month, your finances will have a fairly good income flowing in. This is an opportunity to sit back and receive money with a happy face because money will flow in from many sources from things you have invested and worked hard on, including luck in terms of windfalls. In terms of joint ventures and various investments, there will be a good return.

There is peace within the family. Relatives will still receive help and will help promote your progress in expanding your work or business.

In terms of love, it is ripe and sweet. When many things are in order like this, it is another good time for some people to decide to step into the marriage gate. It is also a good time for asking for love, making up, or going on a honeymoon trip to remember the sweet day.

In terms of health, you can't be careless about car accidents.

Support Days: 2 Oct., 6 Oct., 10 Oct., 14 Oct., 18 Oct., 22 Oct., 26 Oct., 30 Oct.
Lucky Days: 3 Oct., 15 Oct., 27 Oct.
Misfortune Days: 12 Oct., 24 Oct.
Bad Days: 9 Oct., 21 Oct.

Month 10 in the Snake Year (7 Nov 25 - 6 Dec 25)
This month, your horoscope is back to encountering obstacles. The life graph that was rising has dropped vertically. In addition, there are groups of evil stars surrounding your horoscope house. All your responsibilities are not smooth. It is like a storm is coming to pound you, causing obstacles and problems in every

activity, work, and business to have to be constantly solved and taken care of. In addition, there is corruption. The accounting system has bad debts or accounting tampering. What you should do during this period is to work on your responsibilities like a hidden Buddha statue.

If you show up, be careful of being hated. If you show off too much, be careful of being bullied. Therefore, you should take good care of your work. Check your internal accounts and follow up on outstanding debts. Plan your work and documents systematically. Otherwise, you may encounter a crisis.

In terms of finances, this month you will lose money. Therefore, you should not gamble and take risks. Also, do not do illegal business or violate the rights of others because you may be arrested, fined, and prosecuted. For making contracts, during this period, you should consider the details carefully because you may be taken advantage of or have obligations that cause trouble. This month is another month that you must be mindful of. Do not fall for scammers easily. And various investments are not good.

In terms of family, you must be careful of the safety of your family members and be careful of subordinates causing trouble. Health-wise, be careful of illnesses during this period, such as insomnia, gastritis, intestinal diseases, headaches in specific areas, and food poisoning. You should not drive after drinking alcohol.

Love is okay, there are some disagreements as usual, but your lover is very supportive.

Support Days: 3 Nov., 7 Nov., 11 Nov., 15 Nov., 19 Nov., 23 Nov., 27 Nov.
Lucky Days: 8 Nov., 20 Nov.
Misfortune Days: 5 Nov., 17 Nov., 29 Nov.
Bad Days: 2 Nov., 14 Nov., 26 Nov.

Month 11 in the Snake Year (7 Dec 25 - 5 Jan 26)
This month, the road of life moves to the alliance line. In addition, there is a shining auspicious star. Therefore, auspicious energy permeates the zodiac. Many activities that are stuck and seem to not pass will have a better direction of feedback. What you should do on this occasion is select capable personnel who work well together and move forward with their full potential for tangible expansion.

This month's financial horoscope is passable. You will have cash flow from many sources, both income from trading, being a broker, or negotiating a successful business, receiving a percentage of profit. There will also be unexpected fortunes from taking risks and testing your luck.

The career horoscope is a path of prosperity. Work will progress. Business will improve to the point of delight. New investments, if studied carefully and started during this period, will have a good response. Various investments this month have a bright direction.

The family horoscope is smooth. You will receive good news from family members or may have criteria to organize an auspicious event for children. There will be new members. There is also an auspicious date for moving into a new house or workplace. As for relatives, it is smooth. You will find sincere friendship and receive support.

In the love horoscope during this period, the sky is still clear on the side. It is a good time for some couples to ring the wedding bell. There is also an auspicious time suitable for engagement. Married or married, people with good fortune will have peace of mind and good health.

Support Days: 1 Dec., 5 Dec., 9 Dec., 13 Dec., 17 Dec., 21 Dec., 25 Dec., 29 Dec.
Lucky Days: 2 Dec., 14 Dec., 26 Dec.
Misfortune Days: 11 Dec., 23 Dec.
Bad Days: 8 Dec., 20 Dec.

Amulet for The Year of the Monkey
"The Black God of Wealth and Fortune"
(Cai Shen)

Those born in the Year of the Monkey this year should set up and worship the sacred object "The Black God of Wealth and Fortune" (Cai Shen) to enhance their fortune. Place it on your work desk or cash desk to ask for his power and authority to protect you from all dangers caused by inauspicious stars and conflicting forces that you will encounter this year and let them disappear. Only good fortune and wealth will be created throughout the year.

In one chapter of Advanced Feng Shui, it is mentioned that the deities who will come down to reside in the Mie Keng (House of Destiny) of the year. These deities are the deities who can bring both good and bad fortune to the deities of that year. Therefore, worshiping to enhance your fortune with the deities who come down to reside in your birth year is considered to have the best results and have the most impact on you. This is to rely on the power of that deity to help protect you while your fortune is declining and having bad karma to alleviate it. At the same time, ask for his blessing to help your business and trade run smoothly as you wish. Bring glory to you and your family.

For those born in the year of the Monkey, this year is not peaceful. There will be many problems and chaos that you have to constantly gossip to solve. In addition, your birth year is one of the zodiac signs that receives power from the Tai Sui deity. Even though there are supporting stars, overall it is considered a lucky and prosperous year for you. Your career and business will give you, especially good returns if you try to do everything yourself and always keep yourself humble so that you will not encounter any bad events. However, there will still be problems and obstacles waiting in line. Those who do business may have to face fluctuating results. Those who work regularly will feel that their job position is not very stable. In addition, there will be frequent losses of money from unexpected matters. Therefore, please prepare yourself to cope with the situation and find ways to save money. Avoid being a guarantor or partnering with others because it will have negative effects.

In addition, you should be careful with your words and not fall into the trap of ill-wishers, bullying, and being attacked. Also, be careful of adults in the house who may get sick. If you are looking for love this year, it may be a bit dull because some things are beyond your control. In terms of health, be careful of the digestive system. Slipping and falling will cause long-term injuries. If you want to solve and eliminate bad luck and tarnish, you should set up and worship "The Black God of Wealth and Fortune" (Cai Shen) to ask for his power and authority to help you escape all dangers, to have a successful career, to have a profitable business, and to have money flow in. May all your wishes come true. According to Indian beliefs, "The Black God of Wealth and Fortune" (Cai Shen) is considered the god of war and the god who bestows fortune and happiness. It is believed that he is an incarnation of Lord Vairocana Buddha in an angry and fierce form to subdue evil spirits and ghosts. Those who worship him will be protected from all dangers and will experience happiness and success in life as desired in every way. The important appearance of God of the Black Cai Xing is that his skin is black and he has three eyes, which is a manifestation of his power and greatness. The fierce and fearsome face shows determination and bravery (no more hesitation). Standing amidst the flames, which is a symbol of victory that enemies cannot resist. The right-hand holds a high-raised vajra, which is a symbol of using sharp wisdom to cut off the roots of all defilements. The left hand is placed down at the side of the body or sometimes holds other divine weapons, which shows cutting off all defilements and obstacles. In addition, those born in the year of the Monkey should wear a lucky pendant in the shape of "The Black God of Wealth and Fortune" (Cai Shen) around their necks or carry it with them when traveling outside the home, both near and far, so that the person will be filled with auspicious wealth and property, have prosperity and progress in both business and trade and have a peaceful and happy family throughout the year, resulting in better and faster efficiency and effectiveness than before.

Good Direction: Northwest, Southeast, and Southwest
Bad Direction: Northeast
Lucky Colors: White, Yellow, Gold, and Blue.
Lucky Times: 9.00 – 10.59, 15.00 – 16.59, 23.00 – 00.59.
Bad Times: 03.00 – 04.59, 21.00 – 22.59.

Good Luck For 2025